In the Quiet Between Cries

Poems from the First Year of Motherhood

Brittany B. Clements

Contents

Cries

Then You Were Here

And then you were here.

Weeks of trying,
waiting,
testing—
trying again,
waiting again,
testing again.

And then you were here.

Months of back aches,
lightning down my legs.
Nausea, strange sensations,
the constant need to pee.

And then you were here.

Nights filled with
fear,
worry,
excitement,
and whispered prayers.

Days spent cleaning,
decorating,
and preparing—

making space for you.

And then you were here.

Waiting, waiting, waiting.
Hoping.
Anticipating.
Praying.

And then you were here.

Hours of painful contractions,
one writhing wave after another,
after another.

Followed by pushing,
and pushing,
and pushing—

And then,
finally,
you were here.

Meeting You

They lift you
and place you on my tummy,
rubbing you clean with a towel
that's been waiting for you.

"Hi, baby,"
I say, startled by my own voice.
Your dad takes my arm,
guides my hand
to you.

For a moment,
I can't move.

Then—
your heat against my skin,
your weight,
the small certainty of you.

Something in me settles
as you look up at me
and breathe.

It feels so meant to be.

You are ours,
and we are yours.

For forever and eternity.

Every Time

Every time I look at you,
I can't believe it's true.
Here you are,
and you are mine.

Every time I look at you,
I can't believe it's true.
For nine months, you were with me—inside.
And here you are now—my love and pride.

Every time I look at you,
I can't believe it's true.
You are my child.
I am your mother—forever.

Every time I look at you,
I can't believe it's true.
Our family has grown.
Things will never be the same—
for the better.

Every time I look at you,
I can't believe this is all true.

Instructions Not Included

The past thirty-six hours blurred—
ten hours of labor,
painful, challenging, raw,
then the awe of meeting our child
for the first time.

Sleep came in fragments,
if at all.
They showed us how to change a diaper,
wrap the swaddle tight,
and care for the cord.

Then—
before I could fully wake
from my sleepless daze,
clear the fog—
we were discharged.

There we were,
headed home—
baby in the back seat,
no instruction manual.

I guess
we'll learn
as we go.

Night Three

It's 2 a.m. and here we are,
both crying rivers,
your screams echoing
through the silent night.

Your first two nights home,
we took turns holding you
while you slept—
then finally
we found the courage
to lay you in your bassinet.

And you were doing great.

But then something
woke you up.

My fledgling hands
must not have
secured your diaper
tight enough.

And so
here we are.

You're crying—
hungry,

wet.

I'm crying—
sleep-deprived,
self-doubting,
certain I'm failing.

I'm sorry you're wet.
I'm sorry you're hungry.

Please forgive me—
I'm still learning
and trying to give you
my best.

Dear Husband

I'm sorry.
I can't fully know
how this feels for you.

We both brought this child
into the world,
yet he meets us differently—
his reactions
not the same.

The comfort of a mother
comes easily,
instinctive.

But look—
you made him smile,
you made him laugh.

Just like every relationship we hold,
his bond with each of us
will shape and grow on its own.

You may not have
the motherly touch,
but you have *your* touch.

He knows you.

He loves you.

Please know—
I see you.
I feel you.
I send love to you.

I see you
sitting across the room,
anxiously watching it all—
the cameras flashing,
voices cooing,
giggles echoing
down through the hall.

You smile and nod,
trying not to be rude.
But why put in the effort
when they just exclude?

Don't they realize
this baby is here because of you?

You're tired,
hurting,
emotionally beat—

yet all these people gather,
forgetting you might want

quiet,
solitude,
and peace.

I feel you
counting down the minutes
until they all leave,
until you can take back your baby
and retreat.

Because all you want is time
with your precious little one—
yet they are impinging,
focused on their fun.
I send love to you
as you sit there,

holding in tears—
feeling forgotten,
abandoned,
neglected.

You struggle to keep yourself
calm and collected.

What I Didn't Know

I read about pregnancy,
labor,
delivery—

but not about
what comes after.

I wasn't prepared
for the sleepless nights,
nap-trapped afternoons,
hours molded
to the nursery chair,
your mouth
glued to my chest.

I wasn't prepared
for months of nursing pads,
baggy clothes
stained with spit-up,
an appearance unfit
for the world beyond your door.

I wasn't prepared
for the constant needs and attention,
the way my eyes
learned to stay on you,
and my mind too.

I didn't know
what it would be like
when you were finally here.

But I also wasn't prepared
for my heart to grow tenfold.

I didn't know I could feel
so much love,
so deep,
so intense.

Until you were here.

Junk Folder Full

How's the baby?
Can you send a picture please?
How did he sleep last night?
What did the doctor say today?
Is he eating well?
He is so cute!
Aren't you just so happy?

—

All these text messages pop up across my phone.
But what I really need to see is…

How are *you* doing?
Did *you* sleep last night?
Are *you* eating?
Have *you* talked to your doctor yet?
Do *you* need anything?
I'm here for *you*.

I check my inbox
frequently—

more of the same,
less of me.

Attraction

Do you still find me attractive
with my jiggly belly and unwashed hair?

Do you still find me attractive
when it's hard for me to feel pleasure through the pain down there?

Do you still find me attractive
with my breasts off-limits until my supply is dry?

Do you still find me attractive
when I'm emotional and frequently cry?

Do you still find me attractive
with spit-up and drool tainting my shirt?

Do you still find me attractive
when I'm too exhausted to want to flirt?

Do you still find me attractive
with my hormonal acne and sunken tired eyes?

Do you still find me attractive?

Please don't look at me and lie.

You weren't the only one born that day.

The version of me
you call *"Mama"*
was born too.

I know what it's like
for everything to feel new.

In some ways,
I feel just like you—

jolted into a foreign world— *motherhood.*

It's scary.
Confusing.
Unfamiliar.

I imagine you wish
you could return inside me—
warm,
safe,
shielded
from this outside world.

Sometimes
I wish I could crawl back inside myself,

too.

Find the woman I was.

Her world.
One that didn't feel
so fractured.

You and I
are not so different.

As you learn to breathe
outside the womb,
I learn to catch my breath
in the chaos
of motherhood.

<h1 style="text-align: center">In the Quiet</h1>

I wish you could understand
what it's like
to be a new stay-at-home mom.

Some days,
it's a little lonely.

You leave for work—
coffee warm,
keys in hand,
your life still unfolding.

I stay behind,
the door closing softly,
left in the quiet.

I know you carry more now.
I see how hard you try.
I'm grateful.

Still,
I'm a little lonely.

You spend your day
among voices—
meetings,
small talk,

your name spoken.

I spend mine with an infant
unable to speak—
our conversations made of
touch,
rhythm,
need.

Hours pass slowly
with naps,
diapers,
feeds.

Your world expands outward.
Mine folds inward.

I clean.
I cook.
I get ready for bed—

waiting for the sound
of your key in the door,
wanting to hand you my day
the way you hand me yours.

You arrive with stories,
proof the day happened.

I wait for you
to notice mine.

And in the quiet,
after the door opens and closes again—
loneliness stays.

All Touched Out

I lift my shirt
for the eighth time today
and he latches on.

His little hand reaches up,
hooks my lip,
grazes my teeth,
then his tiny finger
makes its way up my nose.

Once that's no longer captivating,
he tugs a chunk of my hair
out from my ponytail
with a relentless grip—
I grimace.

When he's finished,
spit up breastmilk
dribbles down my shoulder,
my chest sticky.

The second I lay him down,
his pupils appear,
and the cry begins.

So I pick him up
and rock

all twenty pounds of him
again.

One After Another

The nights go by one after another—
darkness passes by in a blur.

I wake to your crying
after falling asleep
only hours before.

My head lifts from the pillow,
despite yearning
to sleep some more.

Sleep.
Eat.
Play.
Repeat.

The days go by one after another.
The sun sets faster
than I can keep up.

I forage for a moment to myself
before night arrives once more.

As soon as the sky turns dark,
my mind is spent,
my body sore.

Sleep.
Eat.
Play.
Repeat.

The weeks fly by, one after another,
each running into the next.
One chore finished,
another awaits.

The weekend flickers—
gone—
and Monday returns.

Sleep.
Eat.
Play.
Repeat.

The months quickly escape me,
one after another.

Time slips away.

Some days
the sameness drains me,
my energy wanes.

Sleep.
Eat.
Play.

Repeat—

with repetition,
I begin to change.

Measured Ounces

Will you take this bottle?
Is this the right flow?
How warm do you like it?
How long do I need to put it in the warmer to get it like that?
How come you were fine with it yesterday but screamed today?
How much milk do you take when you breastfeed?
How much should I put in the bottle?
Can I pump enough to satisfy you?
Will we ever figure this out?
Will we get it before I have to go back to work?
What if we don't?

I'll Be There

I promise,
as much as I can control it,
I'll be there.

I'll be there
when you roll the first time.

I'll be there
waiting for you
after your first day of school
in the carpool line.

I'll be there
when you learn to sit.

I'll be there
when you try for your permit.

I'll be there
when you take your first bite.

I'll be there,
when you're scared,
to tuck you in at night.

I'll be there
for your first teeth,

to help you through the pain.

I'll be there
next to you
the first time you ride on a plane.

I'll be there
when you gain your balance
and pull up to stand.

I'll be there
applying sunscreen
as you explore for your first time
in the beach sand.

I'll be there
when you take your first steps.

I'll be there
to help you
with your numerous school projects.

I'll be there
when the doctor gives you all those ouchy shots.

I'll be there
on the other end of the phone line
when you miss me lots.

I'll be there
for your birthdays,

graduations,
wedding—
all the big celebratory days.

I'll be there
on the tough days too,
sharing love
and positive praise.

I'll be there
for all the little things.

I promise,
as much as I can control it—
I'll be there
for whatever life brings.

Between

A Little While Longer

I've never known a countdown like this.

Unlike the one to your due date,
Christmas morning,
or our next vacation—
I want this one to slow down.

Freeze time.

Stay here with you
just a little while longer.
Maybe a little while more.

They say four months is generous,
that maternity benefits are something
to be thankful for.

But it doesn't feel like enough.

Every glance at the calendar,
the space between today
and that dreaded return-to-work date
gets smaller and smaller.

The days close in.
I feel smothered.

How can I leave you?
I don't think my heart can handle it.

Why do I have to leave you?
Maternity leave should be longer.

Do I even have to leave you?
Let's crunch some numbers again.

Time keeps on ticking.

Can I stay here with you
just a little while longer?

You Don't Know, But I Do

I let out a sniffle
as I lift you out of your crib—
you smile up at me,
like I'm the only thing
in your world.

I cry
because to you,
it's just another day.

You don't know
it will be
unlike any other day
you've had.

But I do—
I know.

In an hour,
I'll be back at work,
while you spend your day
with someone else.

Our familiar routine
abandoned.

Our time together

limited—
morning wakeups,
a few brief hours
intertwined with
the rush of dinner,
bedtime chaos,
squeezed spaces
between
weekend errands
and household chores.

You don't know
today will be
different.

And tomorrow
will be too.

You don't know—
but I do.

And so—
as I hold you
this morning
and lay you down tonight,
a tear might fall,
mourning
my once abundant
time with you.

See You Soon

A foreign room.

So many new
unfamiliar faces.

Your little hand
grasps my shirt
just a little tighter,
your head leans
into my chest.

I close my eyes,
breathe you in.

This is it—
it's time to say
goodbye.

But just until
tonight.

I'll miss you
with my whole being—
I know you'll miss me too.

You're going to do great.

Still—
I wish we could turn around,
hit replay
on these last few months.

Scurry back
to the comfort of our home
where it was just us.

Just you and me.
Just you and Mama.

Goodbye,
my sweet baby.
Mama will see you soon.

Pulled Apart

What if you talk
and I'm not there?
What if you walk
and I'm not there?

Returning to work
sometimes
doesn't seem fair.

Please,
please—
I hope
you know
how much
I care.

I don't want to miss
a single thing.

To me,
you mean
everything.

My heart is torn.

I've been with you
every day

since you were born.

Eight hours away
is way too long.
I can't wait
until tonight,
when we're back
together—
where we belong.

Push and Pull

Still do things
for yourself,
they say.

So,
I make that hair appointment,
schedule a spa day.

But every time
I go to leave,
my heart
tells me
to stay.

The push and pull
of motherhood—
the missing
and longing
of staying
and leaving.

I know life must go on,
but you're my
everything.

What I Carry

The dishwasher needs
to be unloaded today.
Two baskets are piled high
with laundry to fold and put away.

I called the vet this morning
and don't forget—
the dog has an appointment
at two tomorrow afternoon.

The grocery list waits until later—
the baby needs to go down
for his second nap soon.

Sometimes I wonder—
what would it be like
to be you?

To have all this
free space
in your head,
without all
the never-ending to-dos?

Sometimes I wish
I could pass it off—
this overbearing

mental weight.

But then again,
I'm not sure
I could
get my mind
out of this mode.

It can be heavy
and taxing,
invisible,
yet important work.

Keeping our world
turning
around
and around,
almost like
clockwork.

The Kitchen Sink

Dry, cracked hands
with peeling cuticles

the pungent smell
of dish soap

splashes of
soapy water
soak my shirt

sore feet,
back aching,
from standing
bent over the sink—

Rinse,
scrub,
rinse,
dry.

Repeat.

Sometimes
multiple times
each day.

Again.

And again.
And again.

They never seem
to dry fast
enough
before
they're needed
again.

Thanks to pumping
and bottle-feeding,
the kitchen sink
and I
have become
close friends.

That Look

That look
you give me
every time I pass
your doorway,

while you play
with your nanny—
wishing it was me.

It pierces my chest,
every time.

My body collapses
to the confusing tugs—

toward you,
where I want to be.

Back down the hall,
my email inbox chimes,
demanding attention.

The endless house chores
beckon me
in yet
another direction.

That look—
stops me cold
in my tracks—
frozen,

immovable,
rooted in opposition.

Only Me

Will you love her
more than me?

No—
how silly would that be?

My thoughts race
anxiously.

I can't let go of
what's worrying me.

Deep breaths…
gain some clarity.

You're his one and only
Mom—
can't you see?

No one
can replace you.
No matter what they do.

Yes—
he will love her
and have fun.

But his love for you
is one
that cannot be
undone.

Time and Space

My energies stretch
in all different directions—
a labyrinthine spider web.

Priorities rearrange
until life's pie chart
surpasses
one hundred percent.

I'm no longer
a stay-at-home mom,
giving my all to my baby.

The separation is tough—
I refuse to work
longer than I must.

These competing priorities
distract me,
diminishing my presence
at home.

I can't shake this feeling
that I can't give anything my best.

I want to give more time and space
to everything

but there's only so much
in a day.

No matter how I delegate
my time and energy,
the clock keeps ticking
precious time away.

I Miss You

I miss slow, conversational dinners,
and Friday date nights out.
Time spent in deep connection
sharing what we dream about.

I miss sitting on the couch,
binge-watching shows
and laughing with you.
Staying up as late as we want,
knowing tomorrow
we have nothing to do.

I miss lazy weekend mornings,
spent cuddled up in bed.
Waking up to sunshine through the windows,
lying next to you—
your chest
a spot to rest my head.

I miss spontaneous trips
to football games,
adventuring through each college town.
Or loading up the kayak on a Saturday,
casting a line,
seeing what fish can be found.

I miss the way things were

before
life was so busy.

Yes—
we see each other
all the time still,
yet I feel
you don't really *see* me.

I miss you, my husband.

Do you miss me?

Undecided

Some days
I want to be a stay-at-home mom,
spend every waking
(and sometimes sleeping)
moment with you,
and never leave your side.

Some days
I want to be able to get up,
leave the house at any given time,
step into freedom,
escape responsibility
for a little while.

Some days
I want to be able to give
all my focus to my work,
advance my career,
without my attention having to divide.

Most days
I don't know what I want,
but I keep telling myself
I don't have to choose
my path forever.

Contradiction

We work to make a living
when our kids are young
and struggle to find time
to spend with our parents
amidst the week's hustle.

When we retire,
our parents are gone
and our kids have grown up
to make a living of their own.

We bring beautiful children
into this world,
then for many reasons
may have someone else take care of them
majority of the week,
forcing us to squeeze
cherished family time
into the weekend,
already filled
with catch-up,
cleaning,
and events.

The few hours of the day
we do get together
are spent getting ready for work;

cooking,
eating,
and cleaning up after dinner;
bath
and getting ready for bed;
and repeat.

Occasionally
I pull myself out of this rat race
and reflect.

Is this really the American family dream?
Sounds like a paradox to me.

Sleep Training

I stare down at your sweet face,
eyes closed,
lips relaxed.

I give you a kiss on your forehead—
"Goodnight baby."

I lower you down into your crib,
bracing myself emotionally
for what's to come.

As your head meets the mattress,
your eyes blink open,
and you smile that charming smile up at me.

"Goodnight baby,
I love you."

The screams commence
before I reach the door.

My body tenses
as I force myself
to turn the knob
and walk out.

I read it only takes a few nights

for the sleep training to work.

With each step
farther down the hall,
I pray it's true.

I don't know
how much more of this
both our hearts can go through.

Helpless

It trickles like a faucet,
the first signs of illness
dripping from your nose.

I try so hard—
saline drops and suction bulbs—
but you throw your head
back and forth in protest.

I don't know
if your throat is hurting,
but I know
you don't feel well.

The way you rub
at your nose and ears,
your pitiful little cough.
I wish I could help you more.

But for now,
I'll just hold you
and pray my love
is enough.

Weathered

When the emotions are pouring down,
the harsh winds of life
whipping through the air I breathe,
and I can't see
through the fog in my brain,

you walk up,
wrap your arms around me,
hold me tight—
your safe shelter from every storm.

As you settle into the space
between my cheek and collarbone,
our bodies melting into one,
the storm stops suddenly.

Once again,
I can feel the warmth
and see the sun.

The tears begin to dry,
the rapid breaths begin to calm
as we sit here,
finding peace and comfort
in the shelter of one another.

Becoming

Becoming

I've shed my old skin.
I feel naked and bare.

The old me is gone,
no matter how hard I search
here and there.

No time for things
the old me would do.

Walk the dogs,
cook special meals,
stay up late just because.

I mourn for my old self,
but welcome the change too.

Because my old self is lost,
but I've discovered
someone intriguing
and new.

Bad Days

Is it just the hormones
or is it something more?

Do I have depression or anxiety?
It's hard to know for sure.

I feel guilt building up inside me,
and lots of embarrassment too.

I can't believe I'm saying this,
but I don't know what else to do.

I feel like something's wrong with me.
This isn't how I pictured it would be.

Do I need medication
or maybe a visit with psychiatry?

Why can't I just feel happy?

I'm trying to give myself some grace.
Remind myself
that everyone adjusts at their own pace.

As I wipe the tears off my face,
I remember I'm not the only mother in the world who has bad days.

Star of the Show

I watch your gaze
bounce from face to face,
as you flash each one
your engaging grin.

You float from one pair of inviting arms
to another,
being passed around
like a decadent dessert
at the holiday table.

You go with it—putting on a show.

I watch,
so proud of you.

Then your eyes meet mine,
and you smile.

A smile different
from all the rest.

Because I'm not just
another one in the crowd.

I'm your one and only "Mama"—
and seeing that loving smile

is the absolute best.

SOS

The saying goes
when a baby is born,
so is a mother.

But learning
this new version of myself
is hard.

My heart yearns
to spend all day with you,
taking care of your every need.

But my mind and internal compass
crave more—
Is that selfish?

I don't recognize
this complex being—
me as a mother.

My thoughts jumble,
feelings whirl—

SOS!

Someone please help me
navigate

this identity crisis.

A Masterpiece

Motherhood is
an ever evolving,
giant, intricate puzzle.

At birth,
all the pieces of you are scattered,
and then you must figure out
how to put them back together,
but the picture looks a bit different
than before.

Some are the same,
some are new,
some are missing,
and some don't fit anymore.

When can you schedule
your workouts?
your daily prayers?
walking the dogs?
the household chores?

How can you make space
for the new pieces
like breastfeeding
and diaper changes?
Where is that old piece of you

that liked to cook and read?

Day by day,
you sift through all the pieces
and click them together
to form the greatest masterpiece—

the new motherly version of you.

Residual

I feel guilty
I didn't see him all day—
he spent it at daycare.

I feel guilty
we didn't get out for fresh air—
I didn't have the energy.

I feel guilty
I didn't read to him—
Ms. Rachel echoes through my head.

I feel guilty
I didn't play with him after work—
I indulged myself instead.

I feel guilty
I didn't get his veggies in
and made mac and cheese for dinner—
the third time this week.

I feel guilty
I didn't get him home in time
for a good restful nap—
his head tilts awkwardly in his car seat.

I feel guilty

I didn't brush his teeth—
it just didn't feel worth the fight tonight.

The list goes on and on,
as I try to convince myself—
plea innocent—
give yourself grace.

What No One Said

I wish someone would have told me
that parenthood is hard—
really hard.

I wish someone would have told me
it's not always
the rainbows and butterflies
society makes it out to be.

I wish someone would have told me
it's okay to feel lost,
like your world is turned
inside out and upside down,
despite something so beautiful
being added to it.

I wish someone would have told me
it's acceptable for your plans to waver—
decisions for the future
cannot
and should not
be made today.

Because
like our babies growing,
things change.

I wish someone would have told me
it was possible for the days
to feel slow,
long,
while still grasping,
desperately,
for more time.

I wish someone would have told me
you don't have to be the old you—
you won't be the old you—
but a new you will blossom
with each passing day.

I wish someone would have told me
it's easy to pretend you don't need help,
but the sooner you get support,
the better you'll feel.

I wish someone would have told me
you're not crazy if you feel
like you are alone
in the deepest, darkest trenches
even while loving
your new ray of bright sunshine
with all you have.

I wish someone would have told me
men and women
process big transitions differently,
adding to the list

of postpartum challenges
and adjustments.

I wish the world would have told me—
but no one did.
These things I learned
with time and experience,
compassion and mercy.

So, here I am
telling you.

Here I am
telling you
that parenthood is hard—
really hard.

But you can do it.
You are doing it.
You will do it.

Because God chose you,
not anyone else,
for your child.

So, here I am
telling you—
even when you feel lost,
exhausted,
confused,
desperate—

You can do it.
You are doing it.
You will do it.

Because
God chose you.

It will get easier.
Some days will still be hard,
really hard—
but you can do it.

Don't let the world tell you you can't.

Dear Fellow Mama—

It may seem you are the only one
up at this time of night,
when the darkness is so quiet
you can hear your every breath,
as you count the stars
outside.

But I promise you are not alone.

There are lights on
in nurseries across the world,
as mothers
wrap their arms around their babies
just a little tighter,
and rock them
a little bit stronger.

You may feel like
you are the only one struggling—
all the pictures make everyone else's
life look grand.

But I promise you are not alone.

Behind each happy picture,

there are moments of tears—
internal battles, challenges, and fears.

It may feel like nobody sees or hears you,
cooped up in the house all day,
surrounded by only baby eyes and ears.

But I promise you are not alone.

You may think
your new normal
is completely abnormal—
that X, Y, or Z is wrong.

But I bet someone reading this
has been through the same.

I promise you are not alone.

Whatever you are thinking
or feeling,
I promise—
you are not alone.

Together

"Let's get together soon."

Followed by days of silence,
sporadic texts,
and often no reply
until the next time.

Gatherings carefully coordinated around naps,
only to be postponed countless times
when illness strikes.

When we finally meet,
the conversations are shallow,
lost over cries and shrieks,
distracted diaper changes and feeds.

One look exchanged
between each other—
the yearning for more,
for closeness,
connection,
and rest.

Friendship in motherhood is tough.

It's the type of thing
only understood by another.

But some harmony comes
from knowing
we're in it together.

Hard to Remember

At first, it feels so foreign
as you learn this new way of life
called motherhood.

After a little while though,
as you adjust to this new normal,
it's hard to remember
what you used to know so well.

It's hard to remember
rolling over in the morning,
the clock reading any time after seven.

It's hard to remember
the quiet and stillness—
just your partner and you.

It's hard to remember
having the independence and freedom
to leave the house,
no little one in tow.

It's hard to remember
going anywhere at all
without at least five minutes of preparation
and a diaper bag about to overflow.

It's hard to remember
date nights that felt so easy—
no plans for a babysitter,
no additional costs.

It's hard to remember
what life was like before
becoming
"Mom."

Life before motherhood
feels like it never existed—
yet these are the wonderful days
that would be hard to forget.

The Reward

A mother's body
grows
another human,
carries it for nine months.

She endures
one of the most physically demanding tasks—
gives birth to a child,
literally giving them life.

A mother heals
while simultaneously taking responsibility
for this new fragile life,
unable to do anything on its own.

A mother feeds her baby,
ensures a dry diaper,
keeps them warm and cool,
provides comfort at any time,
day or night.

A mother manages
the household inventory
of baby supplies
and tiny wardrobes,
updating as seasons pass
and bodies grow.

A mother spends
approximately 1,800 hours
breastfeeding
in the first year—
equivalent to a full-time job.
Some mothers breastfeed
and work a full-time job.

A mother provides a safe space—
a place to retreat,
let any and all emotions loose
at the end of a long day—
no matter how enduring her day was too.

A mother arguably accomplishes
more
than any other role
or occupation.

Yet there's no big medal,
trophy,
award,
promotion,
salary raise—
rarely any external recognition.

But the look they give you
when you enter the room,
their faces light up,
and they scream,

"Mama!"
as they run in your direction
is the best and biggest prize of them all.

Silent Nights

The air feels empty
as my ears strain,
searching for the familiar sounds
of your presence.

Your warm little body
rustling against the sheet,
your tiny chest rising
and falling ever so slightly
with each inhale,
each exhale.

I mourn the closeness
and intimacy we've shared
during these first few months of life.

I hear you cry out
from your room across the hall,
searching for the familiar sounds, too.

Then,
in a few moments,
there's silence again.

And you're sound asleep
in your big boy crib,
in your big boy room.

Collections in the Closet

One by one,
I lay them flat,
run my hand over the soft fabric,
breathe in the smell of baby detergent,
the smell of you.

Some are heavily worn,
a few are faintly stained,
others with small tears in the toes,
a couple with tags still on.

One by one,
I fold them over
shaping small rectangles,
stacking them into piles,
before arranging them in the plastic box.

I lift it up into the closet,
adding to the collection
of containers
with wardrobes
now too tiny
for your quickly growing body.

One by one,
I pack away
a little part of you,

a little part of me,
a lot of sweet memories.

Letting Go, Slowly

I quietly turn the doorknob
and slide between
the door and the frame,
peaking my head around the corner.

And there you are—

arms spread wide,
eyes shut,
peaceful inside
your cozy sleep sack.

I backpedal into the hall
and cautiously close the door.

A tear rolls from my eye
down my cheek,
dropping silently to the floor.

You did it.
You fell asleep all on your own.
But now you need me less.

I raise my sight
over the top of my phone,
poised to take a picture.

And there you are—

standing strong,
standing balanced,
standing tall
on your own two feet.

You flash me a big, proud grin.
I clap my hands
and cheer you on.

You did it.
You stood up on your own.
But now you need me less.

I turn my attention
from my dinner plate,
glance to my right.

And there you are—

sitting proud in your highchair,
stabbing the fork at your food
until some of it sticks,
then clumsily shoveling it into your mouth.

I smile before I can even finish
chewing and swallowing my bite.
I pause,
watching you go at it again.

You did it.
You used utensils to feed yourself.
But now you need me less.

I watch you over and over.

And there you are—

learning and developing,
gaining confidence
and new skills.

The days go by
and I'm awestruck
by your abilities and growth.

You did it.
You achieved the next milestone.
But now you need me less.

Childproof

One day you were stationary on your playmat,
able to wiggle and squirm in one place
but not much more than that.

Before I knew it,
you were up and crawling around,
getting into all sorts of trouble.

I turned my back for a second
and when I looked again,
you had your father's razor in your hand.

*Isn't it crazy how a 10-month-old
can open a drawer so quickly?*

My heart galloped
as I noticed what you held,
the red blood on your pale skin.

Even quicker than you opened the drawer,
I raced to your side.

Somehow you managed to escape
with just a small cut on your pinky.
How lucky we are,
it was nothing more.

I was so mad at myself.
Our house wasn't child-proofed yet.

But then I thought—
neither is the world.

Not every razor will be tucked away in a drawer,
not all drawers will have a lock.

I won't always be just a few steps away
to rush to your side.

But I promise to do my best
to keep you as safe as I can.

Sacrifice and Sustainment

"He barely drank his milk tonight.
I think he's over it,"
whispers my husband
as he joins me in the kitchen,
placing the half-filled bottle on the counter
after putting him to bed.

What he doesn't realize
is the impact of those words.

He can't possibly understand.

One cannot fathom the hours of sacrifice,
the time we dedicate to sustaining our little ones.

The number of electrolyte drinks
and late-night snacks,
plans rearranged
and pumping supplies packed,
aches and pains
and bites endured.

All that work,
time,
commitment,
devotion—
it's hard to believe

when it comes to an end.

Although it means regaining
some freedom and autonomy,
it feels strange thinking
we won't share that experience anymore.

We've ended another chapter,
closed another door.

Wild Child

To my wild one—

I'd be lying if I said
keeping up with you isn't tough.

The truth is,
you completely wear me out most days.

Your curiosity and stubbornness
make redirecting you difficult.

I dread the tantrums
when playtime ends.

Yet you amaze me
with your never-ending energy,
the way you are constantly on the move.

Your shrieks of joy and intrigue
as you explore the world around you.

I can't help but smile as I watch
you indulge in its simple wonders.

Your love for life is contagious.

The world might try to tell you

you're too loud,
too energetic,
too much.

But you will never be too much—
you are perfect the way you are.

The world could use more of
your enthusiasm for life.

Don't let anyone ever
try to tame your spirit.

Stay wild,
my child.

I Thought I Loved You Then

I thought I loved you
when we graduated college
and moved back to your hometown.

I thought I loved you
when you surprised me,
down on one knee,
ring in hand.

I thought I loved you
as I walked down the church aisle,
white dress
trailing behind me,
and said, "I do."

I thought I loved you then.

I never knew I could love you more.

Until—

I saw you hold him
for the very first time,
smiling down
with a warmth
I'd never seen before.

I watched you
change a revolting diaper
despite your extremely wimpy stomach.

I witnessed your impressive creativity—
playing music, bouncing, and being silly—
you tried your best
to comfort him when he cried.

I felt some very scary postpartum emotions.
You held my heart
in the darkest of times
and helped guide me
to the light again.

I've loved you all this time,
but I love the "Dad"
version of you the best.

Another

The way you watch the other children
and your face lights up as you play—
I know you would love a sibling.

Not a passing playmate,
but someone who stays.

Someone to eat breakfast with,
and read stories beside at night,
to grow alongside you—
a forever friend.

Still,
I can't imagine sharing
my love for you
with baby number two.

They say the heart expands.
That love makes room.

But I wonder—

Is my body ready?
Is my mind?
Will you feel replaced,
or will the love multiply?

I want to keep every first—
your words,
your steps,
each version
of who you're becoming.

And yet I imagine
your hand finding another,
the table fuller,
the house even louder.

For now,
I linger
between
fullness and longing,
certainty and fear,
holding space,
love waits.

Big Gray Chair

Even when I'm old
and can't remember anything else,
I think I'll still remember
the back-and-forth motion
of the big gray chair.

I'll remember
the times spent rocking
back and forth,
back and forth.

Your eyes peeking up at me,
affirming your safety,
and your slight smirk
as you doze off into dreamland.

I'll remember
the nights spent rocking
back and forth,
back and forth.

My body glued to the chair,
resisting to put you down
and crawl back into my bed,
despite how exhausted I am.

Instead,

I stay there
with you in my arms,
as we glide together,
back and forth,
back and forth.

I'll remember
the afternoons spent rocking
back and forth,
back and forth.

The sun shining in through the window,
the hustle of the world outside,
while we just sit in that big gray chair,
back and forth,
back and forth.

Even when I'm old
and can't remember anything else,
I'll still remember
the back-and-forth motion
of that big gray chair.

Just Like That

I shut the mailbox door
and pull the red flag up
as the sun beams down into my line of sight
and I squint,
a perplexed, stunned look on my face.

How has a year passed so fast?

It feels like just last month
you were still sleeping
all snuggled up in a swaddle wrap
in your bedside bassinet.

Now you wiggle around
in your sleep sack
in your crib
in your own room across the hall.

How has a year passed so fast?

It feels like just last week
you tasted your first fruit puree,
the majority ending up on your bib
instead of in your belly.

Now you sip water out of your cup
and devour whatever I put in front of you.

How has a year passed so fast?

It feels like just yesterday
you rolled over for the first time,
discovered you could crawl,
and gathered the strength
to pull yourself up to stand.

Now here you are
taking your first independent steps
as you waltz across the room.

How has a year passed so fast?

Just like that—
I'm mailing invitations
to your first birthday party.

Just like that—
our first year together
is coming to an end.

How has a year passed so fast?

A Year to Forever Remember

Despite the challenges,
it's been a year
to forever remember.

A year filled
with cuddles,
snuggles,
and late nights.

Contact naps
and forehead kisses.

A year of growing physically—

lengthening hair,
an expanding belly,
legs and arms stretching longer
and longer.

A year of growing mentally—

learning how
this expansive world works
outside of the womb.

A year of growing emotionally—

forming the deepest bond
between us,
a love I never knew
was possible.

A year of firsts of many—

first smile,
first laugh,
first word,
first roll,
first sit,
first food,
first crawl,
first stand,
first walk.

A year like no other.

A year to forever remember.

<h1 style="text-align:center">One Year</h1>

Today's the day—
the one that marks
the end
of the very beginning.

To you,
it's just another day.
But to me,
it's monumental.

Today's the day—
the one that marks
one year since we became two.

One year since you were born.
One year since everything changed.

One year of the highest highs
and lowest lows.

One year of pure joy,
love,
challenges,
and adjustments.

Today's the day
you become a toddler,

but you'll always be my baby.

115

www.ingramcontent.com/pod-product-compliance
Lightning Source LLC
Chambersburg PA
CBHW070909160726
48004CB00003B/1290